by Rosa Ruiz
illustrated by Diana Schoenbrun

HOUGHTON MIFFLIN   BOSTON

Copyright © by Houghton Mifflin Company. All rights reserved.

No part of this work may be reproduced or transmitted in any form or by any means, electronic or mechanical, including photocopying or recording, or by any information storage or retrieval system without the prior written permission of Houghton Mifflin Company unless such copying is expressly permitted by federal copyright law. Address inquiries to School Permissions, Houghton Mifflin Company, 222 Berkeley Street, Boston, MA 02116.

Printed in China

ISBN-10: 0-618-88644-3
ISBN-13: 978-0-618-88644-9

Hal is tall.
Sal is taller.

Which one is Sal?

Pal is taller than Sal.
He is the tallest.

Which one is Pal?

Kip's tail is short.
Tip's tail is shorter.

Which one is Tip?

Kip has a shorter tail.
Rip has the longer tail.

Which one is Rip?

Matt has a short trunk.
Pat has a long trunk.

Which one is Pat?

Tall, short, long.
Each animal is great.

Responding

Vocabulary

Tall, Short, Long

Draw
Draw 2 dogs. Draw a dog with long ears and a dog with longer ears.

Tell About
Tell someone about your picture. Ask them to draw a dog with shorter ears.

Write Compare and Contrast
Look at pages 2 and 3. Write the name of the tallest giraffe.